THE COMEDY OF HAMLET! (a prequel)

Reed Martin
&
Austin Tichenor

BROADWAY PLAY PUBLISHING INC
New York
www.broadwayplaypublishing.com
info@broadwayplaypublishing.com

Songs: *The Vassal in the Castle* by Austin Tichenor; beats by Zach Moore
In Summary by Reed Martin & Austin Tichenor
In Summary accompaniment arranged & performed by Michael Faulkner
The Plan by Austin Tichenor

Cover art by Lar DeSouza

First edition: November 2023
Revised edition: February 2026
I S B N: 978-0-88145-988-3

Book design: Marie Donovan
Page make-up: Adobe InDesign
Typeface: Palatino

IMPORTANT NOTE

The use of the name

REDUCED SHAKESPEARE COMPANY

in any way whatsoever to publicize, promote, or
advertise any performance of this script
IS EXPRESSLY PROHIBITED

Likewise, any use of the name
REDUCED SHAKESPEARE COMPANY
within the actual live performance of this script
IS ALSO EXPRESSLY PROHIBITED.

The play must be billed as follows:

THE COMEDY OF HAMLET! (a prequel)
by Reed Martin & Austin Tichenor

THE COMEDY OF HAMLET! (a prequel) was workshopped under its original title, HAMLET'S BIG ADVENTURE! (a prequel), at Shakespeare Napa Valley (Jennifer King, Artistic Director), running 3-19 May, 2019. The cast and creative contributors were:

HAMLET, POLONIUS, WEE SCOT VASSAL, SISTER ANGELICA, GRAVEDIGGER, ROSENCRANTZ, FORTINBRAS.........................Peter Downey
THE KING, OPHELIA, LAERTES, SISTER LASCIVIA ....Jessica Romero
YORICK, LILITH, GARKUNKEL, SISTER EROTICA, FREEDOM ....Chad Yarish

Directors ....Reed Martin & Austin Tichenor
Stage Manager .... Mercedes Rivera
Dramaturg .... Kate Pitt
Costumes .... Freya Marcelius
Lighting design ....Keira Sullivan
Props ....Tim Holtslag & Mercedes Rivera
Sound design .... Matthew Cowell
Original circus music ....Peter Bufano
Performed by .... Cirkestra

THE COMEDY OF HAMLET! (a prequel) had its world premiere at the London in Tel Aviv Festival in Israel under its original title HAMLET'S BIG ADVENTURE! (a prequel), running 27-30 November 2019. The cast and creative contributor were:

HAMLET, POLONIUS, WEE SCOT VASSAL,
SISTER ANGELICA, GRAVEDIGGER,
ROSENCRANTZ, FORTINBRAS......................... Doug Harvey
THE KING, OPHELIA, LAERTES,
SISTER LASCIVIA .... Austin Tichenor
YORICK, LILITH, GARKUNKEL,
SISTER EROTICA, FREEDOM ....Chad Yarish

Stage Manager .... Elaine Randolph
Props & Costumes .... Erin Sweeney

Special thanks: Kate Pitt, Jennifer King, Laurence Olivier, Danny Kaye, Tom Lehrer, Lar DeSouza, Christopher Moore, Teddy Spencer, Peter Downey, Jessica Romero, Chad Yarish, Johanne Brøsted, Mya Gosling, Zach Moore, Sheri Lee Miller and the Spreckels Performing Arts Center in Rohnert Park, California, Dee Ryan, and Jane Martin.

CHARACTERS

in order of appearance:

HAMLET
THE KING
YORICK
OPHELIA
LILITH
POLONIUS
WEE SCOT VASSAL
SISTER ANGELICA
SISTER EROTICA
GRAVEDIGGER
FREEDOM
LAERTES
FORTINBRAS
ROSENCRANTZ
GARFUNKEL
SISTER LASCIVIA

CASTING NOTE: Though the original casts comprised only three actors, you're free to use as many actors of any gender or ethnicity as you'd like.

ACT ONE

(Darkness. Wind. Distant thunder. Ghostly howling)

GHOST:
Hamlet….!

(A light rises on young HAMLET. *He's terrified.)*

HAMLET:
Who's there? Stand and unfold yourself!

GHOST: *(Just outside the light)*
Mark me, Hamlet…!

HAMLET:
I will!

GHOST: *(Still in the dark; still ghostly)*
My hour is almost come, when I to
Sulfurous and tormenting flames must render
Up myself.

HAMLET:
Alas, poor ghost!

GHOST: *(Same)*
Pity me not, but lend thy serious hearing
To what I shall unfold.

HAMLET:
Speak; I am bound to hear.

GHOST:
So art thou—to release thy *bowels* when I am near!!

(The GHOST *leaps into the light, wearing a sheet.* HAMLET *screams and tears off the sheet. It's his father,* KING HAMLET. *The lights come up. The spooky sounds cease.)*

HAMLET: Dad!

THE KING: *(Laughing)* Oh Hamlet…I wish you could see thy face!

HAMLET: O God!

THE KING:
So shaken as you are, so wan with care,
Find you a time for frighted peace to pant
And breathe, Hamlet. *Breathe!*

HAMLET:
Can I not to the kitchens for a glass
Of water go without being accosted
By mine own father?

THE KING:
Every time, sweet prince. You fall for it *every time!*

HAMLET:
'Twas not as bad, dear father, as the time,
Whilst asleep, alone in my bedchamber,
My hand you placed in a bowl of warm water.

*(*THE KING *laughs.)*

HAMLET:
Of the bedclothes, there was a great soiling!

THE KING:
When we were boys, I used to do that to
Your Uncle Claudius! So angry was he
That he swore he'd kill me! What canst I say?
Look you, Hamlet, it fits my humor well.
(He gathers up his sheet and throws it offstage.)

HAMLET:
Thou art a lover of practical jokes.

Are there not enterprises of great pitch
And moment the king my liege should tend to?

THE KING:
Don't remind me. Today, and tomorrow and tomorrow
and tomorrow…
You'll know when *thou* becomest king, Hamlet:
Uneasy lies the head that wears a crown.

HAMLET:
Fear not, Father. I shall be ready when
The time doth come, for tis as the song says,
O, I just cannot *wait* to be king!

THE KING:
Be careful what thou wishest for, Hamlet.
To be king, my boy, is no fun at all!
My throne is my prison, and its secrets
Would harrow up thy soul, freeze thy young blood:
The meetings, O God, the endless meetings!
Reading reports, greeting ambassadors,
Executing prisoners, invading countries,
Advisors drone like poison in mine ear!
Maintaining security, waging war,
I barely encounter my wife anymore!

HAMLET:
What wouldst thou be if not King of Denmark?

THE KING: *(Brightening up)*
Oh, I'd be a kid in a candy store
With so many choices in front of me!
I would I had bestowed such precious time
In foreign tongues, or dancing, or fencing,
Stepped on the stage, been a player of parts:
O, had I but simply followed the *arts*!
I could've sung, penned a sonnet or two—
(Realizing)
And *that*, my boy, is what I'd have *you* do!

HAMLET:
Me? No, father, that life is not for me.
I've always known what my path is to be.

THE KING:
Yes, you're single-minded, ready to go;
You're the most decisive young man I know.
But slow down, take your time, think what you do,
There're many options for a boy like you!
Your fate is not fixed inexorably,
Make a choice! Your tale's not a tragedy!

HAMLET:
I *have* made my choice. I will be the king.
Why should I consider another thing?

THE KING:
First of all, I'm the king. You're not the king.
You are barely the prince of anything.
'Twill be many years before you are crowned,
So you should take that time to look around
And see what you like. You're smart as a whip,
I'm sure I could get you an internship!
Perhaps with the Royal Beekeeper—

HAMLET:
The Royal Beekeeper?

THE KING:
Thou couldst assist, help count the colony.

HAMLET:
Two bees or not two bees? *(pause for possible laugh)*
That's your suggestion?

(If [when] the audience groans, THE KING can turn and say:)

THE KING: *(Aside)*
Look, don't pretend you didn't see that coming.
(Back to the scene)
Hamlet, you're young; you have time to explore!

I'll tell you, I've never shared this before,
There's one trade into which I wish you'd go:
(*Checking to see they're alone*)
There's no business like show business, like no
  business I know!
The roar of greasepaint, the smell of the crowd,
The laughter of people you've totally wowed.
When *I* get applause 'tis not worth a thing:
They'd cheer a baboon if he were the king.
I'm an old dog but you're just a pup;
Embrace the childhood I had to give up.

HAMLET:
If 'tis as important to you as't seems,
Why did you choose to abandon your dreams?

THE KING:
There wasn't really a choice to be made;
Father insisted, and—I was afraid.

HAMLET: (*Shocked*)
You?

THE KING:
        Afraid and not allowed to pursue
Things I wanted. I don't want that for you.
You *will* have options that I didn't get.

HAMLET:
Don't control me cuz you're filled with regret!

THE KING:
Looking forward, it would make me so proud
To see you onstage in front of a crowd.
Telling some jokes, perhaps singing a song,
One that would make all who hear sing along.
You deserve glory and fame, acclaim too!
Some day they'll write a great play about you!

HAMLET:
I'm sorry, Father. My answer is—

THE KING: *(Getting an idea)*
Wait! I know just the person who can show
You the ropes and all the tricks of the trade,
Show you how the show biz sausage gets made.
(He goes to the door and claps his hands twice, sharply.)
He's toured the world, he knows how to work it,
Played the whole Scandinavian circuit
From Stockholm to Oslo and Copenhagen to Malmo.
He puts the *oops!* in Uppsala, the sin in Elsinore,
Brings the Lillehammer down and is never stinky in
    Helsinki!
Please welcome the best who keeps getting bester,
The incomparable—

THE KING & HAMLET:
                         Yorick!

THE KING:
                              My royal jester!

(YORICK stumbles in, half asleep. He wears his bathrobe and holds his jester stick, officially known as a marotte but known colloquially here as "L'il Yorick".)

YORICK: You rang?

THE KING: *(Laughing)* Is that how you greet me? I am your king!

YORICK: It's the middle of the night, your majesty! Even a fool needs his beauty rest.

(They laugh.)

YORICK: Not everything I do is a joke, your majesties.

THE KING: Come *on*! Where be your gibes now? Your gambols? Your songs? Your flashes of merriment that are wont to set the table on a roar?

YORICK: They're in bed, where all good people should be.

(YORICK *starts to go but* THE KING *pulls him back by the belled point on his cap.*)

THE KING: Ah-pah-pah-pah-pah-pah-pah… You know my son Hamlet, the Prince of Denmark—

YORICK: 'Course I do! I have borne him on my back a thousand times.

HAMLET: Pick me up again!

YORICK: You are way too big, your highness!

THE KING:
My son the prince has expressed a desire—

HAMLET:
Pretty sure it's your desire, sire.

THE KING: Stop it.
My son will be king, that much is true,
But first, you must teach him all that you do!

YORICK: Any fool can be born a prince, but not every prince is born to be a fool.

THE KING: Not a clown, fool. The boy wants to be a *real* actor!

HAMLET: No, he doesn't.

THE KING: Yes, he does.

YORICK: (*To* HAMLET)
Let me ask this, with extravagant tact:
Who's the idiot who wants you to act?

(HAMLET *points to* THE KING.)

THE KING:
I am, fool, and do not forget your place.

YORICK:
Will he tell truth to power, to its face?

THE KING:
He's having no difficulty so far.
Thus, he should be the kind of man you are.

YORICK:
You want him scrambling for pennies, passing the hat?
Sleeping in stables and eating scraps? That
Is all an actor's able to afford.
I had to *stop* touring, not 'cuz I was bored,
I stopped 'cuz touring does not pay the bills!
Theatre is risky; yes, it's got thrills
But you're always searching for something big:
A solid, steady, reliable gig.
That's why I'm here. It's so fundamental:
A jester's well paid. Plus, I get dental.

THE KING:
Do you even like what you do? At best
You seem a fellow of *limited* jest.

YORICK:
While some other fools are *always* funny,
I'm professional. I do it for money.
I'll have you know, I am a graduate of DADA!

THE KING:
Dada?

YORICK:
The Danish Academy of Dramatic Arts!

HAMLET:
Wittenberg I think's the college for me.
I'll study great leaders and Philosophy!

THE KING:
Your intent with these serious studies
At Wittenberg is most retrograde to
Our desire! We beseech you: college
Is a time of joy, a chance to pursue

All the things you would not normally do.
Join a club, fall in love—

(*Off* HAMLET's *embarrassed reaction*)

THE KING:

                        —or not! Who's to say?
Play a sport, or even be in a play!

HAMLET:
But Father! The thought of being onstage
Terrifies me.

THE KING:

            All the more reason then!

(THE KING *places one hand on* HAMLET's *shoulder and touches his chest with his fist: a distinctive gesture.*)

THE KING:
There is no need for you to be afraid.
You must face your fears; I will not be swayed.

(HAMLET *tries to protest;* THE KING *cuts him off.*)

THE KING:
Children do not always get their own way;
I am the king so you'll do as I say!
You'll study theatre, 'tis my royal decree!

YORICK:
Highness, I think even you will agree:
Nothing's worth less than a theatre degree.

(*A cock crows.*)

THE KING:
Ugh! There it is, the trumpet to the morn.
The castle stirs so I needs must away
To prepare for the business of the day.
Heed me, Yorick. If you fail to comply
You'll kiss your cushy jester job goodbye.
Teach young Hamlet all the secrets you know.

YORICK:
I will.

THE KING:
    Should just take five minutes or so.

YORICK: Hey—!

THE KING: *(Laughing at his own joke then suddenly serious)* Mark me. *(He exits.)*

HAMLET:
O, I've always been so solid and sure,
But now father's made me feel insecure.
What used to be certainty now is doubt.

YORICK:
And *that's* what parenting is all about.

HAMLET:
Then I was right. To Wittenberg I go
To learn what a future leader must know.

YORICK:
Ignoring the king could make our lives grim.

HAMLET:
I'd do it for you, Yorick, but not him.

YORICK:
Just think on't. I know that things are a blur.

(We hear cheerful singing offstage. "Hey, nonny, nonny, hey, nonny…")

YORICK: Here comes Ophelia. You can ask her.
(Turning to go) God, I need coffee. *(As L'il Yorick)* And a danish! *(As himself)* Boy, are *you* in the right place!

(YORICK goes. OPHELIA skips in, carrying a bundle of herbs and a bag.)

OPHELIA: *(Hugging HAMLET)*
Good morrow! How does your honor for this many a
    day?

HAMLET: (*Nervous; re: her flowers*)
Those are nice.

(OPHELIA *thinks he means her chest; now really flustered.*)

HAMLET:
                    I mean, I love your boo—kay.

OPHELIA:
Oh! They're just some things I picked on the way.
There's rosemary, that's for remembrance.
There's rue for you, and fennel, and columbine—

HAMLET: (*Distracted*)
Those aren't flowers. It's an interesting group.

OPHELIA:
No, those are *herbs* 'cuz I'm making a soup.

(OPHELIA *starts pulling items out of the bag and handing them to* HAMLET.)

OPHELIA:
There's potatoes for broth, and carrots for eyesight,
And echinacea as an anti-inflammatory,
And gingko biloba, that's for, uh, memory,
And shark fin, that's for potency—

(HAMLET's *and* OPHELIA's *hands touch. Awkward. She quickly moves on.*)

OPHELIA: (*Pulling out a bouquet of flowers*)
—Oh! And *real* flowers, like
Violets and daisies and roses too…
(*Seeing him not paying attention*)
Hey, Hamlet, what is the matter with you?

HAMLET:
Sorry. I just feel both happy and sad.

OPHELIA:
Was it another debate with your dad?

(*Before* HAMLET *can answer:*)

OPHELIA:
Ugh! Parentals! They doth make me so mad!
We just had two big argument sessions—
Mom won't let me sign up for swim lessons!

HAMLET:
What does your father say?

OPHELIA:
                    Very little.
He *tries* to talk but my mother won't let 'im.

HAMLET: *(Adoringly; he loves his parents)*
My mom worships dad, from the day she met 'im!
They're so much in love, since they were young,
But sometimes she can have a wicked tongue.
She teases my father and makes quite a fuss—
I saw her once kissing Uncle Claudius!
They have such a lovely romantic spark,
Nothing is rotten in the state of Denmark!

OPHELIA:
Promise me, Hamlet, when *we* become parents we
won't—

(Suddenly it's weird.)

HAMLET: *(Embarrassed)*
What?! When *we* become parents? Together?

OPHELIA: *(Embarrassed)*
What? Oh my god! No! Not us two. Never!
I meant, like, when *you* and some other she,
And *I*, and some *guy*, have kids. Separately.

HAMLET:
Whew! That's good, because you're like my *sister*—

OPHELIA:
And you're like my *brother*—

HAMLET:
                          From another
Mister—

OPHELIA:
        Who is from another mother.

HAMLET:
I mean, I *like* you and think the world *of* you,

OPHELIA:
And I *like*-you-love-you but I don't *love*-you-love-you.

HAMLET:
Right. We're better off friends, and friends we'll be!

OPHELIA:
E'en if we live till a hundred and three!

(HAMLET *and* OPHELIA *shake on it, a little too long. They
lean in slightly, then—*)

LILITH: *(Off)*
Fee-Fee!

OPHELIA:
Here comes my mom!

HAMLET: *(Taking out a card and writing)*
                        It's time I disappeared.
I don't like the way she looks at me weird.

OPHELIA:
No, wait!

HAMLET: *(Handing her a note)*
        Here. Read this later! Gotta go!

(OPHELIA*'s mother,* LILITH, *enters as* HAMLET *runs off.*)

LILITH:
Was that Prince Hamlet?

OPHELIA:
                    Yes, mother. As you well know.

LILITH: *(Carefully)*
It's good that you're friends, I'm glad you are close,
But be careful that his favor and affection
Moves not in a more intimate direction.

OPHELIA: *(Embarrassed)*
Mother!

LILITH:
      I'm sorry. Don't be embarrassed, Fee-Fee.
But a boy his age, whatever it may be-be,
Has feelings and urges that are quite hard.
I mean, *difficult* to resist. So they—

(POLONIUS enters.)

LILITH:
Wait, here's your father with something to say.

POLONIUS:
Yet here, Ophe—?

LILITH: *(Interrupting him)*
Your father Polonius is rightly concerned.
Since you've reached your teens, we have watched and
   learned.
You get moody and broody and angsty, it's clear.

POLONIUS:
Moony and swoony—

LILITH: *(Cutting him off again)*
          Be quiet, my dear!
It's perfectly normal. You and the prince
Were children together, but ever since
You two have both…*developed*…

OPHELIA:
          Ew, that's gross.

POLONIUS:
I—

LILITH: *(Talking over him)*
    I'm just saying, you've both been very close,
Like brother and sister—

OPHELIA:
                    That's even grosser.

POLONIUS:
He—

LILITH: *(Talking over him)*
    I'd just hate if you two got too much closer.

OPHELIA: *(Holding it up)*
It's too late, Mother. He wrote me a note!

LILITH: *(Grabbing it)*
What does it say? Let's see what he wrote!

OPHELIA:
No, but—

LILITH: *(Reading)*
"Roses are red
Donkeys pass gas
Don't end up dead
Good luck in swim class!"

OPHELIA: *(Dreamily)*
He's a *poet*! Why must you make this a thing?

LILITH:
Fee-Fee, there's something I just can't tell you,
So don't go falling under his spell! You
Be careful: Before he tries to date you—

OPHELIA:
Oh my god, Mother, I hate you I *hate* you!

POLONIUS:
Ophelia, my dear, the rest is—

LILITH: *(Cutting him off)*
Silence! I pray Hamlet will soon drop thee.

OPHELIA: *(Grabbing the note and exiting)*
I'm learning to swim and you can't stop me!

LILITH: *(Genuinely concerned)*
Oh dear. Children can be such a—

POLONIUS:

                              —burden?

LILITH:
Don't interrupt, dear, I can't get a word in.

POLONIUS:
Sorry.

LILITH:
Shh!

POLONIUS:
Pardon.

LILITH:
Quiet!

POLONIUS:
Apologies!

LILITH:
What did I just say?!
Please, my darling, I don't mean to be shocking,
But you must let me do all the talking.

(THE KING enters, brandishing a pool noodle.)

THE KING:
En garde! Touché! And another French word!

POLONIUS:
Ah! Your highness! How delightfully absurd.

THE KING:
Polonius, is it? I believe Ophelia's your daughter.

POLONIUS:
Her mother hath many times told me so.

(POLONIUS *laughs at his little joke, but* LILITH *laughs way too much. They look at her, confused.*)

THE KING:
Right. As I recall, you're quite close with my brother.

POLONIUS: *(Bowing low)*
I assure you, I've love for no other
But you.

THE KING:
      And your good lady wife? Is she
Likewise devoted and faithful to me?

LILITH: *(Curtsying)*
Lady Lilith Polonius. My love is the same.

THE KING:
That's strange. I thought Polonius was your *first* name.

POLONIUS:
A common mistake, sire. I swear by heaven.

THE KING:
If her name's Lilith, what's your name?

POLONIUS:
                          Kevin.

LILITH: *(To* POLONIUS*)*
Oh, Kevin, go get Laertes ready for school.
I needs must remain and confer with the king.

POLONIUS: *(Bowing)*
As you wish, Dear Lady in Charge of Everything.

(To POLONIUS *as he goes:)*

THE KING:
Good god, man. Don't be led by the nose!
Show her who's boss!

POLONIUS: *(Exiting)*
                 It's all right. She knows.

(POLONIUS *goes. They look around to see make sure they're alone.*)

LILITH:
I'm glad you're here, sire. I've a request—

THE KING:
If it's mine to give, you need only suggest.

LILITH:
'Tis the nunnery, sire.

THE KING: (*Bawdily*)

                Ho-ho! The nunnery, is it?
Why, it's been *years* since we've paid it a visit.

LILITH:
Not *that* nunnery, your most gracious highness.
I mean where girls possessed of a shyness
And devotion to God live in seclusion,
Away from secular manly intrusion,
Free to worship and follow their calling—
Well, the conditions there are appalling!

THE KING:
Sounds like.

LILITH:
      The walls are crumbling, the plumbing's abysmal,
The whole atmosphere's dreary and dismal.
The ceiling is patchy, so's the heating—

THE KING:
It was the sight of our very first meeting,
Full of wonder and magical hocus-pocus—

LILITH: (*Cooly rebuffing his advances*)
Please, your majesty, I need you to focus.
As Chair of the Ladies' Auxiliary, their patron,
I'm in regular contact with the nunnery's matron
Who's never lied in the years I've known her.
She says they need *money*: one thousand kroner.

THE KING: *(Coughing and sputtering)* One thous—!! One thousand—!!

LILITH: *(Calling)* Quick, vassal! Bring some water for the king!

(A WEE SCOTTISH VASSAL, *dressed in a brightly-colored kilt, red beard, and tam o'shanter, runs in with a mug of water.)*

THE KING:
I'm sorry. Say that again. How much do they need?

LILITH:
One thousand kroner.

(THE KING does a massive spit-take on the vassal, who takes the mug and exits.)

THE KING:
                                    That's outrageous! Such greed!
I'm not crazy; that's ridiculous, right?

LILITH:
It is. And they need it by Saturday night.

THE KING:
That's just two days away! Canst thou explain
Why so little in their treasury remains?

LILITH:
Payments, your highness, to settle lawsuits,
And compensate the victims of abuse.
Since then, the nunnery's learned to be wary;
Least they're better than the seminary.

THE KING:
I think the best thing is to just shut it down.

LILITH:
Please! Mighty King, just one jewel from your crown
Can keep them doing Denmark's spiritual work.
With due respect, Hamster, don't be a jerk.

THE KING:
I wish I could help. I'm over-extended:
Too much is on my exchequer depended.
My brother Claudius is such a hassle:
He made me buy him his own new castle!
And Gertrude, my Queen, is keeping me poor
Renovating every inch of Elsinore.
Her contractor has brought me to my knees;
Wood for new cab'nets does not grow on trees!
Plus exchange rates 'gainst the ducat and pound—
I just haven't extra to throw around.

LILITH:
Oh, please, Ham-elot. With respect to your throne,
I love these girls, sometimes more than my own.
They are God's servants; I truly adore them.
And thus I would do anything for them.

THE KING:
Anything, my love?

LILITH:
                              Anything within reason.

THE KING:
Resistance could get you arrested for treason.

LILITH:
Your generosity's what you are known for.
Please. There is so much we have to atone for.

THE KING: *(Seductively)*
What if I knight thee?

LILITH: *(Shocked)*
                              Your majesty! Here?!

THE KING: *(Realizing that's actually a cool idea)*
Yes! You could be Denmark's first lady knight!

LILITH:
Oh my goodness, that would be awesome.

THE KING:

                                   Right?!

LILITH:
My feminine strength I still would display
While kicking some ass in a masculine way.

THE KING:
You'll still be all woman, never a man,
And, as for that money, we'll do what we can.

LILITH:
Then you may do whatever you willeth
With your newest knight, Sir Lady Lilith.

THE KING:
Fantastic! I'm so glad you're on board!
But for this I'll need an actual sword.

(THE KING *is thrown or handed a sword. It's incredibly
heavy and he has trouble controlling it.*)

THE KING:
People forget: I was a dashing sight
When I was a soldier dressed for a fight.
All you have to do is simply kneel *there—*

(LILITH *kneels.*)

THE KING:
And when we're through we'll proclaim everywhere—

(LILITH *stands up, embarrassed, almost impaling herself.*)

LILITH:
Your majesty, you have nothing to prove—

THE KING:
Lady! I can't stress this enough: *Don't. Move.*

(LILITH *kneels again.*)

THE KING:
I dreamt of this while in my orchard nappin'—

POLONIUS: (*Entering suddenly*)
Dear one, if I may…?

LILITH: (*Turning to him*)
                    Darling, please go away!

(POLONIUS *exits.* LILITH *turns back as* THE KING
*accidentally runs her through. She dramatically screams and
dies.*)

THE KING: (*Horrified*)
Good god, that was not supposed to happen.

WEE SCOTTISH VASSAL: (*Off*)
Your majesty—!

(*The* WEE SCOTTISH VASSAL *enters and sees* THE KING *still
holding the sword.*)

WEE SCOTTISH VASSAL:
Your majesty!

(THE KING *takes a beat, then dramatically screams and falls
to the floor.*)

THE KING: (*Improvising*) Begone, you vassal.
Lady Lilith and I are practicing screams—
(*He screams again, and manipulates* LILITH *like a puppet*)
And remembering the days when we were teens
And first saw the Great Yorick! Right, Lily?
(*He nods* LILITH's *head.*)
                    Leave us in our finery.
Begone, wench!

WEE SCOTTISH VASSAL: (*Exiting, impertinently*)
                    I'm a man.

THE KING: (*Calling after him*)
                    Don't be so binary!
(*He lays* LILITH *gently back down*)
Oh, my offense is rank, it smells to heaven!
What am I going to say to Kevin?
Damn these hands and curse this clumsy foil!

Lilith has shuffled off this mortal coil;
Well, to be fair, I shuffled it for her—
Her family now will learn of this horror.
I must conceal this evidence gory
'Til I can devise a good cover story.
(He struggles to drag her off.)
O! My lady, my love for you was great,
But you give new meaning to the term "dead weight".

(They exit. HAMLET enters with an "o what a rogue and peasant slave" intensity, holding a small paper bag.)

HAMLET:
Now I'm confused. I've always felt one way:
That the most important meal of the day
Is breakfast.
(Taking a bagel out of the bag)
        I like a bagel with jelly,
But now the guy at the Elsinore deli
Has just recommended something brand new,
And I haven't a clue what I should do!
(Taking a bialy out of the bag)
To bialy, or not to bialy…
(When/if the audience groans)
The very walls do groan their derision;
Curse you, Father, for this indecision!

(If the audience makes no sound at all:)

HAMLET:
[The very walls do judge me in silence;
Curse you, Father, for this mental violence!]

(OPHELIA enters, wearing swim goggles, a floatie around her waist and/or on her arms, and swim fins.)

HAMLET:
Ophelia! Did you swim or only float?

OPHELIA:
Neither. It was adult swim in the moat.

HAMLET:
That's too bad. Did you talk to your mother?

OPHELIA:
Well, mostly we just yelled at each other.
(Clomping around in her fins)
She's so *unfair* which I do not deserve,
And she totally gets on my last nerve.
What should I do, Hamlet: dance in attendance,
Or assert my maturity and independence?

(HAMLET tries to answer; OPHELIA plows right on.)

OPHELIA:
I'm just gonna do what *I* want instead—
I so hate my mother I wish she was *dead*!

*(The lights change. We hear ghostly wind; maybe there's fog.
HAMLET doesn't notice but OPHELIA does.)*

HAMLET:
Oh dear. Ophelia, I can't be agreeing—

OPHELIA:
Hamlet…? Are you seeing what I'm seeing…?

HAMLET: *(Looking around)*
What do you mean? I don't see anything.

LILITH: *(Off. Ghostly)*
Ophelia—!!

OPHELIA:
Did you hear that?

HAMLET:
Hear what?

(LILITH enters, now transformed into a ghost.)

OPHELIA: *(Gasping)*
Mother…?

HAMLET: *(Not seeing LILITH)*
"Mother"? Ophelia, what's the matter?

LILITH:
Go....away....!

OPHELIA:
No, mother, I cannot leave you!

HAMLET:
You speak to the air, the empty air!

LILITH:
Go....away....!

OPHELIA:
No, mother, no!

LILITH:
Not you—*him!*
To him I am nothing and do not appear;
Send the young prince Hamlet away from here.

HAMLET:
Ophelia, what wild and whirling words do I hear you
    express?

OPHELIA:
Go away, Hamlet, for I must process
These strange feelings. Please do what I say.

HAMLET:
Okay. I won't stay. Come what may, I'll away.
(He goes.)

OPHELIA:
Are you yet living?

LILITH:
I am thy mother's spirit,
Doomed for a certain term to walk these halls
And to be free within these castle walls
To tell thee of my most unfinished—

*(During this, OPHELIA has circled around LILITH, taking
her in. She notices LILITH has stopped talking.)*

OPHELIA:
What, Mother, what? Why are you stopping?

LILITH:
I can't hear myself over your fin-flopping!

OPHELIA:
I wished you dead! A horrible thing to do!

LILITH:
Shh. It is not always all about you.
(Ghostly and mysterious)
But if thou didst ever thy dear mother love—

OPHELIA:
Oh God!

LILITH:
Reeee—

OPHELIA:
—venge your foul and most unnatural murder!

LILITH:
What? No.
(Ghostly and mysterious)
Reee-*place* me as Chair of the nunnery's
Ladies auxiliary.

OPHELIA: *(Horrified)*

          Nooooo! Not a committee!!!

LILITH:
I'm sorry, my dear, I know it's not pretty,
But without your help, the cloister will close.
You must solve their grievous financial woes.

OPHELIA:
Can't we just give them thoughts and prayers?

LILITH:
          Very funny.

No, Ophelia. They need actual money.

OPHELIA:
How can I raise it?

LILITH:
Go to the king. He will help you.
Tell him, as a tribute to your mother,
He must find some money from another
Place and give it to the nuns. He has it
And won't want to lose it. But whereas it
May be hard, you must make him hear it;
Say he *owes* it to your mother's spirit.
He has more than enough money to spare,
He just needs to be persuaded to care.

(POLONIUS *enters, right next to* LILITH, *who he neither sees
nor hears.*)

POLONIUS:
Ophelia! Hast thou seen my good lady wife?

OPHELIA:
I—

LILITH: (*Amazed*)
    He doesn't yet know that I've lost my life!

OPHELIA: (*Answering her father*)
—have not.

POLONIUS:
            Last I saw her, I left her with the king.

LILITH: (*To* POLONIUS)
What did you see? Did you see anything?

POLONIUS:
Fee-Fee, did I hear you talking to someone?

(LILITH *gestures to* OPHELIA *not to say anything.*)

OPHELIA:
No, my lord. Not a living soul.

POLONIUS:
I've something to say—

LILITH:
I wish you wouldn't!

POLONIUS:
You're your mother's daughter and still quite young—

LILITH:
Oh god, here he goes.

POLONIUS:
        Around her, give thy thoughts no tongue—

LILITH:
Be quiet.

POLONIUS:
        Let thy behavior be nobly shaped—

LILITH:
The bottle's uncorked and the genie's escaped!

POLONIUS:
Let me share what has been made clear to me—

LILITH:
Noo—!

POLONIUS:
      —just how much your mother is dear to me.

(Beat)

LILITH:
Sorry what.

OPHELIA:
        Thank you, Father. She's dear to me too.

POLONIUS:
Please let her know if she appears to you
Before I find her.
(He exits.)

OPHELIA:
        Well, that's sweet to say.

LILITH:
Even a stopped clock is right twice a day.

OPHELIA:
Mother! Why do you hate my father so?

LILITH:
I don't hate him, Ophelia. It's just, you know,
I'm ashamed of my own behavior, and
My shame says what it will rather than
Confront the devil in mine own vile heart.

OPHELIA:
Mother! What have you—?

LILITH: *(Cutting her off)*
                              You have to be smart,
Smarter than me.

*(LILITH tries to take OPHELIA's hand but can't grab it.
Ghostly wind sound)*

LILITH:
                    Please, do not be seduced
By the glamour of royalty. Get used
To your own power, and try to be wise,
And always remember you are the prize.
Marrying a prince makes you a princess,
And nothing on earth do I want for you less.
Don't be mindless, vapid; that isn't you.
Remember: To thine own strong self be true.
The secret, Ophelia, is really no mystery:
Well-behaved women rarely make history.

OPHELIA:
Oh Mother—!

*(OPHELIA tries to hug LILITH's ghostly form but can't.
Ghostly wind effect)*

OPHELIA:
                    I can't believe that you're gone!

LILITH:
I know, but you'll have to keep moving on.

(They try to touch hands but are unable to during this next couplet).

Since my powers are greatly diminished,
You must complete my business unfinished!
Be not concerned with how my life ended;
'Twas an accident most unintended
And mustn't distract from the task at hand,
Which is to make your—I mean, the king—understand.
Get thee to the nunnery! Save it now!
Or at least by Saturday night.

OPHELIA:
                                    I vow!

(LILITH is suddenly jerked, then drawn backward.)

LILITH:
Oh dear, it seems my time is drawing nigh.

OPHELIA:
No! I just cannot bear to say goodbye!
Mother, will we never again be met?

LILITH: *(As she's being pulled off)*
Who knows? I'm not sure how this all works yet—!

(LILITH is gone. HAMLET enters.)

HAMLET:
Ah, good! Ophelia—

(Notices OPHELIA staring:)

HAMLET:
                          Are you all right?
Sorry to bother; I need your insight.

OPHELIA: *(Shocked; in a daze)*
I need to go.

HAMLET:
Ophelia, thy goggles are all un-straight,
No swim cap upon your head, thy floaties
Down-gyved to thy elbows. Art thou late for swim
  class?

OPHELIA: *(Noticing her gear and pulling it off)*
What? Oh, no. I'll have to give that a pass.
I must find the king.

HAMLET:
What's the matter? You look like you've seen a
Ghost.

OPHELIA: *(As she exits; absently)*
Do I?
(She exits, still in shock.)

HAMLET:
Oh dear. She seems not well. But I require
Advice and assistance.

(YORICK enters.)

YORICK:
  Greetings, young sire!

HAMLET: *(Excited)*
The very man! I need wisdom and vision.

YORICK:
Good luck with that. How goes the decision?

HAMLET:
I've spent all morning sifting gold from bronze,
Examining all of the pros and cons,
Weighing the strength of my father's suggestion—
To be an actor, or not to be an actor, that is the
  question.

YORICK:
Was it suggestion or more a command?

HAMLET:
That's exactly what I don't understand!

YORICK:
Well, you still will be king: That much is true.
But I think your dad thinks, what *else* can you do?

HAMLET:
You think I should be a player like you.

YORICK:
Slow down, chief. There's no rush to begin this.
I need to be sure you're in this to win this
And be certain quite you've no doubt of it.
Hamlet, do you think I could talk you out of it?

HAMLET:
Absolutely!

YORICK:
            Then you're not an actor!

HAMLET: *(Sulking)*
What to my father dost think I should say?

YORICK: *(Getting an idea)*
Hang on. We should have a play. Extemporé!

HAMLET:
What? Why?

YORICK:
            It's a way to practice your thinking—

(As HAMLET slumps:)

YORICK:
And to stand strong and tall without slinking.

HAMLET: *(Reluctantly)* Fine. Do thou stand for my
father and examine me upon the particulars of my life.

YORICK: I shall!

*(YORICK assumes a kingly posture and gestures for HAMLET
to begin.)*

HAMLET: Greetings, Father.

(YORICK *gives* HAMLET *a look; he can do better than that. As the scene continues,* HAMLET *loosens up and begins to enjoy himself.*)

HAMLET: I mean, your majesty!

YORICK: (*Scolding his "son", imitating the actor playing* THE KING) Hamlet, my son! I do marvel at thy foolish desire to follow in my footsteps! Thou shouldst live out my boyhood fantasies and not be doomed to become Denmark's king! Fortunately, Hamlet, thou art oft accompanied by a court jester, a gifted, accomplished, *genius* of a man, a goodly dashing fool, i' faith; of most unlimited jest, who can teach you his quips and quibbles, and is so damned sexy as to make everyone he meets feel tingly in their naughty bits. But what was his name…?

HAMLET: Yorick.

YORICK: I'm sorry?

HAMLET: Yorick.

YORICK: One more time for the people in the cheap seats!

HAMLET: Yorick!

YORICK: Yes, his name is Yorick! There is virtue in that Yorick; stick with him!

HAMLET: (*Getting into it now*) Okay, thou dost not speak like a king. Let me try! Do thou stand for me, and I'll play my father.

(HAMLET *and* YORICK *switch places, each imitating the actor playing those roles.*)

HAMLET: (*As "The King"; deep-voiced kingly grandeur*) Now, Hamlet…!

(YORICK *kneels on the floor and poses heroically but speaks in a high-pitched boyish voice.*)

YORICK: Hi Dad!!

HAMLET:
The complaints I hear of thee are grievous. What's this I hear about you behaving sensibly and responsibly? It's most disgusting for a boy your age. You should be into games and mischief, not politics and statesmanship!

YORICK: *(Sulking baby voice)* But I don't like play-acting! I want to be miserable, Father, like you!

HAMLET: *(As* THE KING*)* And I want you to live the life I never had!

YORICK: *(Whiny baby* HAMLET*)* I can't make up my mind!

HAMLET: *(As* THE KING*)* Ungracious boy! *Unfortunately*, there is a jester that's always hanging around, a play-acting bald-headed jackass of a fool, that huge bombard of jokes— *(change bald-headed to whatever best describes your actor)*

YORICK: Uh-huh.

HAMLET:
That stuffed cloakbag of bits—

YORICK: Accurate.

HAMLET: That roasted turducken with ham in his belly—

HAMLET & YORICK: —Yorick!!

YORICK:
You know what, Hamlet? Your father's correct:
You have a talent I didn't expect.
But your father's more goofy, less stuck-up—

HAMLET:
Oh please. Now you're just being a suck-up.

YORICK: No, he's more— *(Striking a pose)* Wow, look at
me! I'm the King!

HAMLET: No way! He's like— *(Striking a pose)* I'm the
King so you'll do as I say!

YORICK: *(Posing)* No, I'm the King!

HAMLET: *(Posing)* No, I'm the King!

*(THE KING enters, nervous and distracted, and sees their
mockery. HAMLET and YORICK notice him and drop to their
knees, scrambling to bow the lowest.)*

THE KING: Well, I'm glad *somebody's* the King.

YORICK: A thousand apologies, your highness.

THE KING: Rise. There'll be no punishment, no cursing;
I'm just glad to see Hamlet rehearsing!

YORICK: *(Eager to apologize and redeem himself)*
Majesty, he's *good*! With you I'm agreed:
His pretend greatness is greatness indeed!

THE KING:
That's nice.

YORICK:
The boy has talent; he may have the will
As well, and know how to go out and *kill*!

THE KING: *(Blurting out)*
I didn't kill anyone!

YORICK: *(Confused)*
        No, I mean, when you "kill" or "die" onstage,
You can still live to a healthy old age.

THE KING: *(Covering)*
Right. That's what I meant.

YORICK:
Although—there was that time, your highness,

When the great Sir Thomas of Cooper—
(He takes his hat off in respect.)

THE KING:
Ohh, yes—

YORICK:
                    —that fool of renown
And wit didst collapse to the floor, struck down
By an attack of the heart—but the crowd didn't know.
They thought his collapse was part of the show!

THE KING:
Death haunts us all. What a horrible blow.

YORICK:
Are you kidding? 'Twas a great way to go!
Onstage, in his prime, geared up for battle,
Every cowboy wants to die in the saddle.

HAMLET:
So an actor's career's uncertain at best.
Your job's on the line, you're put to the test—

THE KING:
Just like a king! We have no stability!
We fight off threats to the best of our ability,
Like fratricide and assassination—
To be in a play would be a vacation!

HAMLET: *(Defiantly)*
I'm decided then. I have made the call.
One way or other, death comes for us all.
And since my father here's clearly shattered,
I want to have lived doing what mattered.
At the risk of you feeling the loss of me—
(Deep breath)
I'm off to Wittenberg to study philosophy!

THE KING:
Help me, Fool! Won't you speak up a minute?

YORICK:
What's the point? His heart's clearly not in it.

HAMLET:
I've made my choice, Father. I'll spend my days
Learning to lead and not playing in plays.
(HAMLET *holds* YORICK'*s chin, in the same way he'll one day hold his skull.*)

HAMLET: (*To* YORICK)
I don't mean to harass, poor Yorick.
(*They take a beat and look at the audience, allowing them to laugh.*)
No offense.

YORICK:
        None taken.

THE KING:
I think you're mistaken!
If that's your choice, I'll try to accept it,
(*Starting to go*)
But as for my love, do not expect it.

HAMLET:
But—

THE KING: (*Stopping*)
        Oh! Find Ophelia. She needs a friend.
(*Starting to go again*)

HAMLET:
What? Why?

THE KING: (*Stopping*)
            Her mother has reached a sad end.
(*He tries to leave again.*)

YORICK:
Good lord.

HAMLET:
            What happened?

THE KING: *(Stopping; reluctantly)*
                    A tragic event:
Killed…in a…freak—needlepoint accident that I had
nothing to do with.
Her family's sobs will go right through you;
I'll find Ophelia and send her to you.
(He exits.)

HAMLET:
Ophelia and I both lost parents today.

YORICK:
Well…she in a slightly more permanent way.
I'm reminded by this awful report:
Don't waste your life, Hamlet. It's short.

HAMLET:
Father hates me! I'm the saddest of men!
I'm never making a decision again!

YORICK:
That's actually a decision…

(OPHELIA enters, cutting him off.)

OPHELIA:
Hamlet! Help me!

HAMLET: *(Embracing her)*
I'm so sorry what happened today!

OPHELIA:
Yes, mother died but—*she won't go away!*

(HAMLET and YORICK look at each other. OPHELIA presses on.)

OPHELIA:
She appeared to me, a pale apparition,
And she spoke to me and gave me the mission
Of completing her work and raising money
To save the nunnery—

YORICK: *(Laughing bawdily)*
                    Ho ho!

OPHELIA:
                         That's not funny!
Mother's nunnery is not a whorehouse!
And the nuns will end up in the poorhouse
If we can't raise funds to save the convent.

HAMLET:
Okay, we'll help you. You're clearly in need.
(To YORICK*)*
Right, Yorick? We'll do what we can?

YORICK: *(Reluctantly)*
                              Agreed.

HAMLET:
I'll ask my father. He'll give you money.

OPHELIA:
I already did. He just looked at me funny.

YORICK:
He's terrible with money. Like many
Kings he wastes it so he never has any.
All the new gadgets he just has to own,
Like those fancy cup holders for his throne,
Gold-plated toilets, novelty socks,
His brand-new catapult's still in the box!
Plus, he's too generous. There's always another
Present to buy for his wife and his brother.
What we need's a special one-time event—

OPHELIA:
That people will pay for! A lot of them, too.

HAMLET:
But what could that be? What can any of us do?

OPHELIA:
Maybe Yorick can entertain the folks.

YORICK:
You can't afford *my* killer jokes.

OPHELIA:
Not you alone, but perhaps with the prince—?

(They turn on him.)

HAMLET:
Oh no no no! You will never convince
Me.

YORICK:
    Yes, that could work. "For one night only!
The Prince of Denmark, all by his lonely!
Singing and dancing! A comedy! A lark!"

HAMLET: *(Protesting)*
That'd be "The *Tragedy* of the Prince of Denmark".

YORICK:
Your highness, the people will pay to see you.
And you were quite good in our little play;
So now be the hero and save the day.

OPHELIA:
You're not a servant under indenture,
Come on, it'll be a big adventure!

YORICK:
And it's not like this is a lifetime thing:
You can still be your philosopher king!

HAMLET:
I can't do this alone. That'd be terrible.

YORICK:
Yeah, it would. One-man shows are unbearable.

HAMLET:
And what if something goes wrong? What then?

YORICK:
It's not really a question of *if,* but *when.*

HAMLET:
What?!

YORICK:
      Things *will* go wrong 'cuz things always do.
The mark of your greatness is how well you
Acknowledge what happened and find your tongue;
You can't unring a bell once it's been rung.
Respond, tell the truth, and make it your thing;
That marks a great actor, and a great king.

HAMLET:
But kings work alone. I hope that's my fate.

YORICK:
Tyrants work alone. Leaders collaborate.
I'm telling you, spending time in the theatre
Will help make you a much better leader.

HAMLET:
How?

YORICK:
      Theatre teaches teamwork, empathy,
Public speaking and flexibility,
Discipline, creative problem solutions,
Time management, conflict resolutions,
Critiquing others knowing you're better—
How big a flask you can hide in your sweater—
Subsisting on ramen and minimum wage
Are all things you'll learn on the wicked stage.

OPHELIA:
We'll make it an epic pageant about life here in
Elsinore, but I know not what to call it.

YORICK:
Titles are hard.

HAMLET:
Our Castle!

YORICK:
No, that makes it seem like it's about a building. This is about the people in our little community. *Our Town!*

HAMLET:
Our Village?

YORICK:
Our Hamlet!

OPHELIA:
Or, make it a musical—*Hamleton!*
(Striking the pose)
Work!

(Music kicks in, a dramatic pulsing beat.)

OPHELIA:
But we gotta be careful. Look what we've got:
My mother's been killed, it could be a plot
To keep the nunnery closed forever and ever.

HAMLET:
Who would want that? Who would be that clever?

OPHELIA: The vassal in the castle.

HAMLET: What vassal in the castle?

OPHELIA:
The vassal in the castle tryna blow up the show.
That Scottish laddie is a baddie looking guilty in his
     kilty
With a rocket in his pocket make the room go BOOM!

(Music vamps; OPHELIA *continues:)*

OPHELIA: Look around, look around, we'll be lucky if we can stay alive right now.

HAMLET: I think you're being paranoid…

OPHELIA: Fortunately, I have a neighbor who used to sail on ships.

HAMLET: Okay…

OPHELIA: Now she locks people up and is both an excellent poet and a great swordswoman.

HAMLET: Great!

OPHELIA: But be careful when you meet her. She gets nervous around new people and is always worried she's improperly dressed.

HAMLET: Okay, that's a lot of *incredibly* specific information. Let me see if I have this straight—

(The beat kicks in again)

HAMLET:
There's a vassal in the castle who's a laddie and a
    baddie
With a rocket in his pocket tryna to blow up the show.

OPHELIA:
Right.

HAMLET:
He'll be lurking where we're working but your
    neighbor with a sabre
Who's a sailor and a jailer has some skill with a quill.

OPHELIA:
Exactly! But!
Pay attention! I should mention there's contention and
    dissension
From the sailor and the jailer who is filled with
    apprehension.

HAMLET:
Is it better if I let her change her sweater than forget her
And defend her like a friend, or just pretend I never
    met her?

OPHELIA:
My position is: Tradition gives you loads of
    ammunition,
On condition you're not fishin' for permission to

audition

A magician or musician who is skilled in composition!

HAMLET:

I'm just wishin' my ambition to be king and politician
Didn't find such opposition from my father's
  prohibition.

OPHELIA:

Yeah, he stated that he hated royal fate that you
  awaited—
Wait! This show that we create will leave him sated
  and elated!

HAMLET:

On this morning I do thank you, though I warn you I
  outrank you,
I am willing and attentive and it's thrilling!

OPHELIA:

My incentive is I do not want more killing *and I do not
  want to spank you*!

HAMLET:

Got it.

*(Musical sting [rehearsal audio, video, and performance
backing tracks available at BroadwayPlayPublishing.com])*

YORICK:

Wow—that vassal in the castle?

OPHELIA:

Yeah?

YORICK:

What an asshole.

OPHELIA:

Right?

HAMLET:

This pageant must occur! It will restore
My bond with my father, whom I adore.

I say to you now that the play's the thing
Wherein I'll catch the *affection* of the king!

OPHELIA:
We will have to rehearse both day and night.
We need this money by Saturday.

YORICK:

Right!

HAMLET:
I might have some tiny skill with a lute.

YORICK:
You're the prince: Whatever you do will be cute.
Okay, let's see what I can do. Hamlet,
Do you have today's *Elsinore Gazette*?

(HAMLET *hands him a sheet of newspaper, which* YORICK *unfolds and holds up.*)

YORICK: Ophelia, please examine this piece of newspaper.

(OPHELIA *examines it.*)

YORICK: Actually, let's ask someone else. (*Calling to the booth*) Can we have more torches lit in the castle!

(*The house lights come up.*)

YORICK: Excellent. (*He picks a person in the audience*) Can you examine this piece of newspaper? Is it of a single piece?

(*They answer in the affirmative.*)

YORICK: I will now tear it into several pieces. (*He does.*) I will now compress these several pieces into a ball and place them in my closed hand like this. Now I will ask you all to wave your hands in the air and say the magic words after me. When you have done so, before your very eyes a miracle and most welcome sight will appear. Are you ready?

(They answer; he demonstrates)

YORICK: Okay, everybody! "Abracadabra—"

(They repeat the word.)

YORICK: "You're a sexy magician –"

(They repeat it.)

YORICK: Hey, thanks, you guys, that's really nice. "Now it's time for—"

(They repeat the phrase.)

YORICK:
"A brief—*Intermission!*"

(They repeat the phrase as YORICK unravels the balled-up newspaper—it now has the word "Intermission" in bold letters on it [this is a fairly easy magic trick to learn, just search "Torn and Restored Newspaper" on YouTube]. As the audience applauds:)

OPHELIA:
Yorick, everybody!

HAMLET:
We'll be back in fifteen minutes!

OPHELIA:
This is gonna be great—!!

(They run off.)

END ACT ONE

ACT TWO

(OPHELIA *enters.*)

OPHELIA: Royal subjects and friends of the court, welcome to tonight's fundraiser to save the Elsinore nunnery! (*She pimps applause.*) I'm so glad so many of you could make it, there must be literally tens of people here tonight. It's been a hectic couple of days putting together tonight's entertainment, but we were happy to do it because nothing— (*Almost overcome, but controlling herself*) —nothing was more dear to my late mother's heart than the Sisters of Perpetual Suspicion. I'd like to invite two of the sisters up here to join me. Please welcome Sister Angelica and Sister Erotica!

(*Two* NUNS *enter. One of them carries a guitar.*)

EROTICA: Thank you.

ANGELICA:
We'd like to thank you all for coming out tonight to save the nunnery.

EROTICA: Speaking of coming out, I don't see any of our priests here tonight.

(ANGELICA *and* EROTICA *both laugh at their wickedness.*)

ANGELICA: I'm so nervous. I'm no good at oratory.

EROTICA:
I'm great at oratory!

(ANGELICA *and* EROTICA *laugh again, hysterically.*)

ANGELICA: By the way, do you know how to get a nun pregnant?

EROTICA: Dress her up as an altar boy.

(ANGELICA and EROTICA laugh again, followed by a big sigh.)

ANGELICA: Anyway. All of the proceeds from tonight's ticket sales will go towards ongoing costs of maintaining our convent. *(She "oohs" while playing syrupy "Save The Children"-type music.)*

EROTICA: But ticket sales alone can't cover everything. We'll happily accept any donations you want to give. Any kroner you can spare will be greatly appreciated. Just a few pfennig a day will make a huge difference in the lives of these children of God. But we'll take any currency you have: kroner, mark, franc, pound—

ANGELICA: —even nun dollars and nun cents!

(ANGELICA and EROTICA laugh.)

EROTICA: We love that joke.

ANGELICA: What kind of sense of humor do we have?

ANGELICA & EROTICA: Nun!

OPHELIA: Okay, ladies, that's enough jokes.

EROTICA: Sorry, it's just a habit!

OPHELIA: *(Wagging her finger)* Ah-ah-ah! Ladies, this is all too complicated. Let's just make it easier for everybody to understand—

(ANGELICA plays an arpeggiated G7 or E7 chord, depending on the key.)

OPHELIA: Bless you, sister. *(Singing slowly, earnestly, almost operatically:)*

   C/A
In summary
        Am/F#m
Let's save the nunnery!

       C /A   Am/F#m
It needs some money, bring the funny,
        Dm7/Bm7   G7/E7
Raise some dough!

ANGELICA & EROTICA: *(Singing)*
Ah-ah-ah!

OPHELIA:
      G7 / E7
We'll be theatrical
     C / A
Ecclesiastical,
    Dm7/Bm7
I say a play within a play's
        G7/E7
The way we'll go!

ANGELICA & EROTICA: *(Singing)*
Please don't go! Ah—!

OPHELIA:
  F/D
Hear our entreaty:
  A7/F#7
These nuns are needy
  Dm7/Bm7
And we'll succeed, indeedy,
    G7/E7
Speedy greed will make it right

ANGELICA & EROTICA: *(Singing. Bending the harmony like a barbershop quartet)*
Make it rye-eye-ight!

OPHELIA:
      C/A
That's how in summary
       Asus7 –> A7/F#sus7 –> F#7
We'll save the nunnery!

                Dm7/Bm7   G7 /E7
We are so righteous that we might just
        C/A
Win tonight!

(The ladies curtsy and ANGELICA *and* EROTICA
exit. [Rehearsal audio and video available at
BroadwayPlayPublishing.com])

OPHELIA:
Sisters of Perpetual *Hilarity*, am I right? Be sure
to catch their regular set every Friday night at the
Elsinore Chuckle Hut. But now, tonight's variety show
fundraiser features some of the best talent Elsinore has
to offer, as well as this next guy. Of all the performers
in tonight's show, he is certainly one of them. Please
try to drum up some enthusiasm for the allegedly
comic stylings of Mr. Delver, the Gravedigger!

*(*OPHELIA *exits as the* GRAVEDIGGER *enters.)*

GRAVEDIGGER: *(In a Cockney accent)* Good evening,
ladies and germs! Like the little lady said, I'm Delver
the Gravedigger. You may have seen me around, and
if you don't know me yet, well—people are dying to
meet me! *(Laughs at his own joke)* Tell you a little about
meself. What is he what builds stronger than either the
mason, the shipwright, or the carpenter? The grave-
maker, for the houses he makes last till doomsday!
(Laughs) Hmm. Tough tomb. It's important to have
someone like me here tonight because let's face it, a
show like this either kills or it dies. Either way, I'm
burying something! In fact, there's a lot of death in my
family. And when *I* go, I want to be buried in a glass
coffin. Will it happen? Remains to be seen.

*(*YORICK *has entered with a flagon of rhenish to see this*
disaster. He pours it on the GRAVEDIGGER'*s head.*

GRAVEDIGGER: *(Sputtering but delighted)* A pestilence on you for a mad rogue, sir! I do like a bit of physical humor.

He kneels on the floor to wipe up the spill.

YORICK: How long have you been doing stand-up?

GRAVEDIGGER: Thirty years, man and boy.

YORICK: And how long have you been a gravedigger?

GRAVEDIGGER: Thirty years, man and boy.

YORICK: Wait, how old *are* you?

GRAVEDIGGER: Thirty years, man and boy.

YORICK: Oh–kay. You can go.

GRAVEDIGGER: God bless you, sir! G'night, everybody! Don't forget to tip your serving wenches! *(Exits)*

YORICK: Delver the Gravedigger, everybody! Do *not* quit your day job. I want to give a special shout-out now to one of our sponsors: Dunkin Danish. Because Danes Run On Dunkin. And now we have a very special guest, all the way from England, please give it up for a very special member of the gentry, Sir John Falstaff!

(As YORICK *speaks, he curves around left and exits as* OPHELIA *enters curving right, holding a clipboard. We're now "backstage".)*

OPHELIA:
Where is he? There's still so much to be done!

*(*YORICK *enters, having just been "onstage".)*

YORICK:
Okay, where's Hamlet? The show has begun!

*(*HAMLET *enters, nervous.)*

OPHELIA:
There you are! Your absence gets me so vexed!

HAMLET:
I know, I'm sorry—

YORICK:
                    Come on, you're on next!

HAMLET: But I've set down a speech of some dozen or
sixteen lines. We could insert it—

OPHELIA:
What?! A speech?! You want to add something new?!

HAMLET:
Don't go crazy, Ophelia, let me show it to you—

OPHELIA:
Hamlet, we don't have—

(HAMLET *drops to one knee, and starts Acting with a capital
A. Lots of gestures, big faces, and huge emotions*)

HAMLET: (*Loudly and over the top*)
How all occasions—!

YORICK / OPHELIA: Shh!!

(*All remain wary of being too loud backstage.* HAMLET
barely quiets.)

HAMLET:
—do inform against me
And spur my dull revenge! How stand we, then, that
Have a father rejected, a mother killed,
The imminent ouster of the whole cloister
That for the want of one thousand kroner—!

(YORICK *and* OPHELIA *are horrified by what they're seeing.*)

YORICK:
Stop! Please stop! All that emotion's distracting.
They give awards for *Best* Acting, not *Most* Acting.
But it's a good trick to pull out of your hat;
Ever want people to think you're insane? Do that.

HAMLET:
It's good you're a fool. You're no diplomat.

YORICK: *(Sincerely)* I'm sorry. It was the single greatest performance I've ever seen.

HAMLET: Really?

YORICK: No, *that* was acting!

OPHELIA: Shh!!

YORICK: It offends me to the soul to hear a robustious, periwig-pated fellow tear a passion to tatters, to very rags. Pray you, avoid it.

HAMLET: *(Bowing sarcastically, gesturing extravagantly)* I warrant your honor.

YORICK: Nor do not saw the air too much with your hand, thus, but use all gently; for in the very torrent, tempest, and, as I may say, whirlwind of your passion, you must acquire and beget a temperance that may give it smoothness.

HAMLET: *(Waving his arms)* I thought that's what actors do.

YORICK: *(Waving his arms)* No, that's what *bad* actors do. Don't just do something—stand there. Was that even English?

HAMLET: Of course.

YORICK: Why? *We speak Danish!!*

OPHELIA: Can I remind you, the show has already started?! And we still need someone to play Fortinbras.

YORICK: Falstaff's almost finished and then it's you. Let's see the love scene.

OPHELIA: *(Together)* Uhh...

HAMLET: *(Together)* Well...

YORICK: You haven't rehearsed your love scene?!

OPHELIA: I've been very busy putting this show together!

HAMLET: And I've helped!

YORICK: The best part about theatre is rehearsing love scenes!!

OPHELIA: What about all that stuff you said earlier about leadership and conflict resolutions?

YORICK: Fuck that. Show me the scene.

(YORICK *takes the clipboard.* HAMLET *and* OPHELIA *reluctantly "act", she doing too much and he doing too little.*)

HAMLET: (*As Romeo, stiffly*)
If I profane with my unworthiest hand

(OPHELIA *takes* HAMLET'*s hand.*)

HAMLET:
This holy shrine, the gentle sin is this:
My lips, two blushing pilgrims, ready stand
To smooth that rough touch with a tender kiss.

(OPHELIA *puts her hand up to* HAMLET'*s mouth. He kisses his own fingers then touches her hand.*)

OPHELIA: (*As Juliet, badly*)
Good pilgrim, you do wrong your hand too much,
Which mannerly devotion shows in this;

(HAMLET *and* OPHELIA *turn to each other.*)

OPHELIA:
For saints have hands that pilgrims' hands do touch,
And palm to palm is holy palmers' kiss.

(OPHELIA *grabs* HAMLET'*s palms with hers. He can't avoid it.*)

HAMLET: (*As Romeo*)
O then, dear saint, let lips do what hands do.

(OPHELIA *puckers her lips but* HAMLET *kisses the air.*)

OPHELIA: And—scene.

YORICK: What are you doing?!

HAMLET: Nothing.

YORICK: I can see that! But you should probably do *some*thing!

HAMLET: You just told me *not* to do something.

YORICK: Well, be not too *tame* neither! Suit the action to the word, the word to the action! You gotta do this justice! It's one of the most famous love scenes in history: *Romeo and Juliet* by the famous Italian author Matteo Bandello!

OPHELIA: It's my fault, I'm not an actor.

YORICK: Have you ever pretended to be interested in your parents' advice?

OPHELIA: Of course.

YORICK: Then you're an actor. Listen—
Here's the secret, which I'll tell you for free:
You don't need *to Act*, you just need *to Be*.
I mean, come on, I shouldn't have to mention
You two are dripping with sexual tension.

OPHELIA:
Woah! Inappropriate!

HAMLET:
                          Soo out of line.

YORICK:
Okay, I get it. You're virgins, that's fine.
It's called a *play*, but if you overdo it, it looks like *work*.
Anything so overdone is from our purpose of playing,
which is to hold, as 'twere, the mirror up to nature.
Keep it simple, keep it real, make the audience go "woah".

(YORICK *gestures in such a way that the audience goes "woah".*)

HAMLET / OPHELIA: Woah.

YORICK: Yeah, like that! And remember to keep it fun! *(To* HAMLET*)* Your father likes fun! You want to please your father.

HAMLET: *(Sulking)* He's not coming. I tried to invite him to the performance and he wouldn't even see me.

YORICK: Okay, you're clearly not ready. I'm gonna bump you down in the lineup, closer to the end. I'll move that trio of singing sisters up next.

OPHELIA: Who are they?

YORICK: They call themselves Nuns and Roses.
(He starts to go then stops)
You know what? This. I've missed this! The chaos,
The madness of folks who put on a show,
Who develop a closeness and think they know
Their love is the stuff of timeless romance!

(HAMLET *and* OPHELIA *cringe in embarrassment.* YORICK *puts his arms around both of them to buck them up.*)

YORICK:
Fear not! Your love's what we call a *show*-mance.
Forged in the fire of heaven & hell,
Love found in rehearsal never ends well.
The tale will turn grim for both thee and thou—
(He breaks the spell)
But not tonight! We've a show to do now!
Good luck! Don't suck!
(As he exits "onstage")
Sir John Falstaff, everybody—!
(He goes.)

OPHELIA: *(Making awkward conversation)* So—Is your mother coming?

HAMLET: No! She's gone to Vejlefjord, for the waters, with my Uncle Claudius for some reason. I don't want her here anyway, it's going to be terrible.

OPHELIA: Hamlet! It's *not* going to be terrible. Yorick's right. We just need to have fun.

(In OPHELIA's *attempt to cheer* HAMLET *up, she's gotten very close to him, which they're now both suddenly aware of. She starts to say "I love you" but catches herself in time.)*

OPHELIA: I lo…iterally have to find someone to play Fortinbras. *(As she goes)* I'll look in the kitchens. Maybe someone there knows how to speak Norwegian.

*(*OPHELIA *exits.* HAMLET *practices some of his Romeo & Juliet gestures. Ghostly wind sounds and lights)*

LILITH: *(Off. Ghostly)* Ophelia! Ophelia! *(She enters and notices* HAMLET.*)* Oph—for the love of god, it's you.

*(*LILITH *is invisible to* HAMLET.*)*

LILITH:
Hello…? You still can't hear what I say.
Oh, I wish I could make you go away!

*(*LILITH *gestures innocently on her line, and* HAMLET *suddenly spins in a circle. Wind noise)*

HAMLET: Woah! What happened?

LILITH: Did I do that?

*(*LILITH *gestures again, and* HAMLET *spins back in the other direction. Wind noise)*

LILITH:
I've only been dead for forty-eight hours
But I have acquired some awesome powers.

*(*LILITH *bats* HAMLET *around like a ping-pong ball. Wind noise accompanies each move.)*

HAMLET:
If this stuff happens before every show,
Into theatre I don't want to go!

LILITH:
I've had my fun, but away with you now.

(With a gesture, LILITH whisks HAMLET offstage.)

LILITH:
I need to find my Ophelia somehow.

(THE KING enters, excited to be backstage.)

THE KING:
Being backstage is as cool as it seems!
Fin'lly, Hamlet is following my dreams!

LILITH:
The last person you're expecting to see,
Hamburger Helper, I'm guessing—
(She gestures and makes herself visible)

           —is me.

THE KING: *(Seeing her, horrified)*
Thou rise again! The graves have yawn'd
And yielded up their dead! I am *really*
Sorry for killing you.

LILITH:
Not as sorry as I am.
Have you seen to where our children have gone?

THE KING:
I have! I've hidden and spied on the lad
'Cuz I want him to think that I'm still mad.
They've been rehearsing their love scene—

LILITH:
                    Their what?!

THE KING:
Yes! It's adorably grownup; well, somewhat.

I'm so sorry it's a thing you're missing
But they hold hands and I think there's some kissing—

LILITH:
No no no. That's not what I want to hear.
Oh, Fee-Fee! I thought I made myself clear!

THE KING:
Why? What's the matter? It's only pretend.
Would the Prince make such a rotten boyfriend?

LILITH: *(No choice but to reveal this)*
The fair Ophelia, whom your son adores,
Is not Polonius's daughter. She's yours.

THE KING: *(After a beat)*
Whaaaa—

LILITH:
            I thought it best if you never knew
But in my present state there's naught I can do.

THE KING:
Good god! Let not the royal house of Denmark be
A couch for luxury and damnèd incest. This isn't
    England!

LILITH:
They're young, in love, an affair of the heart—

THE KING:
Nonetheless—

LILITH:
                —yes, we must keep them apart.

THE KING: *(Trying to apologize for killing her.)*
Can I find mercy?

LILITH:
                    Well…it would be best
If you saved the nunn'ry. Grant her request!
Go! You must raise the cash quickly somehow.

THE KING:
I will, one way or another. I vow!

(THE KING *exits*. POLONIUS *enters*.)

POLONIUS: (*Searching for her*)
Ophelia—?

(LILITH *gestures and appears to* POLONIUS.)

LILITH:
    Husband?

POLONIUS: (*Terrified*)
        Ahh!

LILITH:
          I have a request.

POLONIUS: (*Catching his breath*)
I should've known that your spirit can't rest.
O Lilith fair, we do miss you a lot,
Are you—happy?

LILITH:
        No, I really am not.
Ophelia and the prince, is't true what I hear?

POLONIUS: (*Excited*)
It is! They're putting on a show!
Ophelia gets it from me, you know;
If you recall, you once had the knowledge,
I was a bit of an ac-*tor* in college—

LILITH:
Oh my god, stop! Are they having an affair?

POLONIUS:
Not yet, but I believe love's in the air!

LILITH:
I need you, right now, to put a stop to it.
I'm clearly in no position to do it.

POLONIUS:
But why? I wouldn't know how to begin.
To marry a prince is hardly a sin.

LILITH: *(Deep breath)*
I regret to say, one can't help these things,
Ophelia's not your daughter. She's the king's.

POLONIUS:
Whaaaa—

LILITH:
She's still the same girl, she's not another.
Don't blame her for the sins of her mother!

POLONIUS: *(Slowly; processing)*
But she isn't mine, from what I can tell.
Still, I will try to love her passing well.
I will raise her, feed her, make her my chore,
But there's no doubt I'll love Laertes more.
Unless you have more surprises for me—?

LILITH:
No, it was just one time.

(POLONIUS looks skeptical.)

LILITH:
                         All right, twenty-three.
If you neglect or leave her unfulfilled,
I will return and ensure you are killed.

POLONIUS: *(Turning to go)*
I'm leaving.

LILITH: *(Desperate)*
              You'll be thought wise and respected
But you will die when you least expect it.

POLONIUS:
Say your goodbyes, if you can, because then
Your name will never be mentioned again.
Ophelia may cry, and she may resist it,

But 'twill be as if you never existed.
(Exits)

LILITH:
Relying on men leaves too much unknown;
I might have to handle this on my own.

(LILITH exits. The Ghostly lights disappear.)

(OPHELIA enters, we're now "onstage".)

OPHELIA:
Friends of the nunnery, I've been checking the tally,
and right now it appears we're a little behind pace
to reach our goal of raising one thousand kroner so
please give generously to the nuns holding donation
baskets in the lobby. Give till it helps. And I want to
remind you we have some delicious snacks on sale in
the lobby: Ableskiver, Kanelsnagle, and Weinerbread,
which you know what, tastes much better than I
expected. All right, we have a very special treat for you
now—

WEE SCOTTISH VASSAL: *(Crossing upstage of the doorway)*
Here, boy!

OPHELIA: *(Going on)* Next up in our performance
tonight is someone I know you're all going to love—

*(The WEE SCOTTISH VASSAL enters whistling, as if for a
dog.)*

WEE SCOTTISH VASSAL: Freedom…! *(Whistles)* Freedom!

OPHELIA: *(Terrified)* Begone, you vassal in the castle! I
won't let you blow up the show!

WEE SCOTTISH VASSAL: I never wanted to blow up the
show! I want to be in it! But I need to find my pet! *(He
holds up a "Missing Person" poster. It shows the Loch Ness
Monster.)* Freedom!

OPHELIA:
Your pet is the Loch Ness Monster?

WEE SCOTTISH VASSAL: Ssshhh! He dinnae like to be called a monster. I will search on! Freedom! Freedom!

OPHELIA: Why do you keep saying that?

WEE SCOTTISH VASSAL: That's his name. *(Calling)* Freedom!

OPHELIA: Give me that—!

(Music begins. OPHELIA takes the poster and exits. YORICK enters in a comic Loch Ness MONSTER outfit, carrying a chair or stool. He sits and files his nails.)

WEE SCOTTISH VASSAL: *(Delighted)* Freedom!

(WEE SCOTTISH VASSAL holds up a small treat. The MONSTER puts out his hand as if to say, "Give me the treat." The WEE SCOTTISH VASSAL indicates that the MONSTER should beg like a dog. Extremely reluctantly and with a lot of attitude, the MONSTER begs and the WEE SCOTTISH VASSAL gives him the treat. The WEE SCOTTISH VASSAL bows and gets applause.)

(Now the WEE SCOTTISH VASSAL offers another small treat. The MONSTER puts out his hand for the treat. The WEE SCOTTISH VASSAL indicates that the MONSTER should roll over on the floor. Again with extreme reluctance and a lot of attitude, the MONSTER stands and rolls over. The WEE SCOTTISH VASSAL gives him the treat and the MONSTER sits again. The WEE SCOTTISH VASSAL bows and gets applause.)

(The WEE SCOTTISH VASSAL now grabs a hoop and indicates that the MONSTER should jump through it. The MONSTER is reluctant. The WEE SCOTTISH VASSAL sets a tube of Haggis-flavored Pringles on the far side of the hoop and again indicates that the MONSTER should jump through. The MONSTER stands and very deliberately walks downstage of the hoop, picks up the Pringles, crosses back to his chair, and sits. The WEE SCOTTISH VASSAL places the hoop over the head of the MONSTER and sets it around the base of the

chair onto the ground. WEE SCOTTISH VASSAL *bows and gets applause.)*

*(*WEE SCOTTISH VASSAL *now notices the* MONSTER *eating Pringles and decides he is hungry and would like a chip. He puts out his hand asking for a Pringle. The* MONSTER *indicates that the* WEE SCOTTISH VASSAL *should beg like a dog. The* WEE SCOTTISH VASSAL *begs and the* MONSTER *gives him a chip. The* MONSTER *bows and gets applause.)*

(Now the WEE SCOTTISH VASSAL *puts out his hand asking for another chip. The* MONSTER *places a single chip on the floor and holds the hoop between the* WEE SCOTTISH VASSAL *and the chip, indicating that the* WEE SCOTTISH VASSAL *should jump through the hoop. The* WEE SCOTTISH VASSAL *runs up to the hoop, stops, and slowly steps through the hoop. He picks up the chip and eats it. The* WEE SCOTTISH VASSAL *and the* MONSTER *bow together. Just as the bow finishes, the* WEE SCOTTISH VASSAL *grabs the whole tube of Pringles from the* MONSTER *and runs offstage with the* MONSTER *in pursuit.)*

YORICK / MONSTER: *(As he runs off)* Get back here, you monster!

(The WEE SCOTTISH VASSAL *runs back across the stage one final time, holding the Pringles can triumphantly.)*

WEE SCOTTISH VASSAL: *(As he runs across)* Freedom!! *(Rehearsal audio and video available at BroadwayPlayPublishing.com)*

(The lights change and THE KING *sneaks on. We're backstage.)*

THE KING:
Hamlet…? Hello…? Are you here anywhere?
What a terrible falling out was there.
He asked to see me and I declined him
But now I want him and I can't find him!

*(*YORICK *enters and sees* THE KING.*)*

YORICK:
Your highness! I'm so glad you could make it!

THE KING:
I feigned disinterest but can no longer fake it.
Where are Hamlet and Ophelia?

YORICK:
They're just about to do their big love scene.

THE KING:
Noo! They can't do that!

YORICK:
                              Why? What do you mean?
They will make a great missus and mister!

THE KING:
I just found out they're brother and sister.

YORICK: Whaaaa—

THE KING: It's a long story.

YORICK: Does your wife the Queen know?

THE KING: No! And you mustn't tell her! Fortunately Gertrude's away; I couldn't go so I sent my brother Claudius with her!

YORICK: I'm not sure that's a great idea—

THE KING: We have to hurry! You look that way, I'll look this way—!

(THE KING *exits one way.* YORICK *starts to exit the other way, but* HAMLET *enters.*)

YORICK: Hamlet!

HAMLET: Not now, Yorick, I've got to introduce Laertes.

YORICK: But I just saw your father—

HAMLET: *(Cutting him off)* My father? He's here?!

YORICK: Yes, and he's very upset. He said—

HAMLET: Of *course* he's upset! He's still angry that I'm daring to live my own life and make my own decisions!

YORICK: No, that's not it. He said—

HAMLET: I don't care what he said, Yorick! Go get your sound effects. You and Laertes are on next.

(HAMLET *exits through one door and enters through another, coming "onstage" and leading applause.* YORICK *tries to grab him but he can't, so he exits.*)

HAMLET: Okay, royal subjects and special guests, right now I want to introduce to you the son of the woman we remember tonight, Ophelia's brother, Laertes!

(LAERTES *enters, intense, as* HAMLET *exits one way.* YORICK *enters the other way, carrying a small table of sound effects equipment. The original production used a slapstick, bike horn, duck call, slide whistle, ratchet, flexitone, crow bar, and metal pipe. You can find a rehearsal video of what this looked and sounded like at the BPPI website.*)

LAERTES: Thank you, two people. The Prince of Denmark asked me to give a demonstration of swordsmanship. But since my own mother, Lilith Polonius, was very recently the victim of an accident involving sharpened steel, I'm going to do something a little different.

(LAERTES *unsheathes an imaginary sword from an imaginary scabbard.* YORICK *makes the ZZING! of metal against metal.*)

LAERTES: I've just returned from France where I have mastered—

(LAERTES *flips the imaginary sword between his hands three times as* YORICK *makes whish sounds*)

LAERTES: —the art of mime! As you can see—

(LAERTES wobbles the blade as YORICK makes a noise with a Flexitone.)

LAERTES: I have sworn off swords— *(He pronounces the W)* I mean, I've sorn off sor—dammit! *(Carefully)* I swear I have sores!

YORICK: Ew.

(LAERTES swipes the sword; YORICK makes a the swishing sound:)

LAERTES: Real blades are far too dangerous.

(LAERTES swipes again; YORICK makes the sound.)

LAERTES: The only reason we can't have sensible blade laws is because of the NRA—

(LAERTES swipes again; YORICK makes the sound.)

LAERTES: —the National Rapier Association! So with the help of Yorick, I am going to recreate for you now the historic battle between good King Hamlet, played by me, and the evil King Fortinbras of Norway!

(FORTINBRAS enters, looking exactly like the SWEDISH CHEF, swishing an imaginary sword.)

SWEDISH CHEF: Herndy ferndy nerndy burndy herndy ferndy nerndy swords up yours!

LAERTES: *(To YORICK)* What did he say?

YORICK: He said, "Neener neener neener, I can pronounce *swords*. Up yours."

LAERTES: How dare you! En garde sir!

(LAERTES swings his "sword" again and the SWEDISH CHEF parries it with his own imaginary sword. We hear the CLASH! of steel against steel made by YORICK.)

(They fight, with increasing ridiculous moves and sound effects. Finally, they drop their swords and take out imaginary lightsabers and fight with those, with YORICK making the sounds. Then, Jedi-like, LAERTES gestures with

his free hand and the SWEDISH CHEF's *lightsaber goes flying. Then he chokes the* SWEDISH CHEF *from a distance, saying:)*

LAERTES: I find your lack of herndy ferndy disterndy.

*(*LAERTES *snaps the* SWEDISH CHEF's *neck. They all bow.)*

ALL THREE: Thank you!

*(*YORICK *strikes the sound table as the other two run off.)*

YORICK: Give it up for Laertes, folks! We have a very special treat for you now: The *actors* are come hither! They are the best actors in the world, either for tragedy, comedy, history, pastoral, pastoral-comical, historical-pastoral, tragical-historical, tragical-comical-historical-pastoral, scene indivisable, or poem unlimited…

(As YORICK *says this, he turns his focus to the wings and exits, as if the audience is swinging its focus backstage.* OPHELIA *enters, tallying up the figures on her clipboard.)*

OPHELIA: I'm so relieved that vassal in the castle turned out not to be a hassle. Carry the one… Ugh! We need a boost if we're going to reach our donation goal. I don't want to do this but we might have to send in the mimes to do a silent auction.

*(*ROSENCRANTZ *enters, a guitar around his neck, followed by another man [*GARFUNKEL*] in a Bob Ross wig.)*

ROSENCRANTZ: Excuse me—

OPHELIA: You can't be back here. Can I help you?

ROSENCRANTZ: Well, we're in Hamlet's fourth-period study hall and he told us we can perform tonight. We're Rosencrantz—

GARFUNKEL: —and Garfunkel.

OPHELIA: Are you singers?

GARFUNKEL: Yes. Well, we're actors too.

ROSENCRANTZ: We were in a play by Sir Tom of Stoppard.

OPHELIA: *Travesties*?

GARFUNKEL: No, we were pretty good.

OPHELIA: Well, what can you sing?

(ROSENCRANTZ *plays and they sing:*)

ROSENCRANTZ & GARFUNKEL:
Hello, Hamlet, my old friend
We've come to sing for you again—

OPHELIA: Stop! No! I'm afraid there's no room on the program.

(ROSENCRANTZ *and* GARFUNKEL *sing again, angrily.*)

ROSENCRANTZ & GARFUNKEL:
Ophelia!
You're breaking my heart!
You're shaking my confidence daily—!

OPHELIA: *(Grabbing his guitar)* No! I'm sorry, please go!

(ROSENCRANTZ *and* GARFUNKEL *exit, fighting as they go.*)

GARFUNKEL: This is your fault, you know.

ROSENCRANTZ: My fault?! You're nothing but a haircut!

GARFUNKEL: You know what I need from you? A few more sounds of silence.

ROSENCRANTZ: Why I oughta—

(ROSENCRANTZ *pulls* GARFUNKEL's *hair. It comes off in his hand.* GARFUNKEL *screams and exits.*)

ROSENCRANTZ: I knew it!! You're not even a haircut! I'm telling you right now, we're through! Rosencrantz and Garfunkel are dead!

(ROSENCRANTZ *exits.* OPHELIA *puts the guitar on a stand down right and checks her clipboard.*)

OPHELIA: Okay, what's next…? Oh my god, my love
scene with Hamlet! Okay, now, don't be nervous, don't
be nervous… *(Vocal warmups)*
The tip of the tongue the teeth the lips,
The tip of the tongue the teeth the lips,
Here we gooooo—
*(She exits through one door and comes out the other, as
if both doors are the opposite sides of the same door. Now
"onstage")* —kay, everybody! It's the moment I've
all been waiting for! Hamlet, the Prince of Denmark
himself, making his stage debut in the love scene from
that famous Italian romance, *Romeo…and…*

*(OPHELIA probably doesn't get to finish this as YORICK
enters, trying to get her attention.)*

YORICK: Psst! Ophelia!

OPHELIA: *(To the audience)* I'm sorry. *(To YORICK)* Not
now, Yorick!

YORICK: *(Whispering)* You can't do this scene!

OPHELIA: *(Whispering)* No, it's okay. It'll be great!

YORICK: *(Whispering)* Hamlet can't kiss you!

OPHELIA: *(Whispering)* He better kiss me!

YORICK: *(Whispering)* No!

OPHELIA: *(To the audience, going right on)* Here he is,
please welcome Hamlet, the Prince of Denmark!

*(OPHELIA gestures to one doorway and YORICK leaps in
front of it to stop him, but HAMLET enters through the other
doorway and joins OPHELIA downstage. YORICK lingers in
the archway, afraid to interrupt.)*

*(We hear the familiar ghostly wind noise. The lights
change. HAMLET doesn't notice but OPHELIA looks around
nervously.)*

OPHELIA: Mother?

HAMLET: *(As Romeo)*
If I profane with my unworthiest hand—

(HAMLET tries to take OPHELIA's hand, as before, but now they can't seem to grasp each other.)

HAMLET: *(Struggling)*
This holy shrine, the gentle sin is this:
My lips, two blushing pilgrims, ready stand
To smooth that rough touch with a tender kiss.

(HAMLET tries to kiss OPHELIA's hand, but can't. More wind noises.)

OPHELIA: *(As Juliet)*
Good pilgrim—

(OPHELIA pulls her hand away and HAMLET smacks himself in the face.)

OPHELIA: *(To the air)*
Mother!
(To HAMLET)
                        —you do wrong your hand too much,
Which mannerly devotion shows in this.
(Struggling to grasp his hands)
For saints have hands that pilgrims' hands do touch,
And palm to palm is holy palmers' kiss.

HAMLET: *(As Romeo)*
O then, dear saint, let lips do what hands do.

(Now HAMLET and OPHELIA try to kiss lip to lip, but they can't come together. YORICK watches, fascinated from the archway.)

OPHELIA: *(Still puckering)* Mother—! Stop interfering—!!

(Ghostly wind sound as HAMLET and OPHELIA go flying apart. Pushed by invisible hands, they're shoved together center stage. Then they're each spun to face downstage. They both bow, awkwardly, then are shoved offstage in opposite directions.)

OPHELIA: *(As she exits)* Mother!!

*(*YORICK *moves down center, covering. He wears a fez.)*

YORICK: Okay! Ophelia and Hamlet, doing it *just* like they rehearsed it! I'd like to do for you now my impression of good King Hamlet juggling his affairs of state. *(He names three juggling balls as he pulls them out)* Taxes! Diplomacy! And War! *(He juggles them, ad-libbing as necessary. He finishes with a big ta-da! Wiping off sweat)* Thank you. I owe it all to the man who inspired me, the legendary fool Sir Thomas of Cooper. He made me the fool I am, and I wear this fez as a tribute to him. *(He puts his hand to his chest.)* Ow. I've had a pain here all night. *(He reaches into his coat and pulls out a small [plastic] pane of glass.)* There's the pane. Not one of my better ones— *(Looking through it)* Clearly.

*(*YORICK *chucks it into the wings. We hear glass breaking.)*

YORICK: *(Pulling a marshmallow out of his pocket)* For my next trick, I will make this marshmallow disappear and you will erupt into completely spontaneous thunderous applause. *(He pops the marshmallow into his mouth. He gestures for the audience to react.)* Thank you! Now watch very carefully as I use my mystical and borderline useless abilities to conjure a live dove out of thin air. Just like that! Nothing up this sleeve. *(He makes an elaborate gesture.)* Nothing up the other sleeve... *(He pats the other sleeve hard and feathers fall out from his cuff. He looks at the feathers and decides to move on as if nothing has happened.)* For my final trick I will use my amazing magical bag. You can see as I turn the bag inside out that nothing is inside. But something amazing will happen if I wave my hand and have you repeat after me. Abracadabra—

(The audience repeats it.)

YORICK: *(Suddenly feeling genuinely ill)* I don't feel well—

(The audience repeats it.)

YORICK: No, I really don't feel well—

(If they repeat it again, YORICK can say:)

YORICK: Read the room, people. Not everything I do is a joke!

(HAMLET and OPHELIA hover in the doorway, seeing that something is wrong.)

HAMLET: Yorick, what's the matter?

YORICK: I'm dying up here—

HAMLET: No, you're doing great!

YORICK: *(Struggling to join HAMLET in the door)* Ask for me tomorrow and you shall find me a grave man. *(He clutches his chest again.)*

HAMLET: What is it? Say something!

YORICK: *(Clutching HAMLET)* Goodnight, sweet prince. Cut me in quarters and cover me with jam…

HAMLET: Why?

YORICK: I'm…toast…!

(YORICK dies. HAMLET lets him down gently to the floor, mostly offstage. OPHELIA and HAMLET are horrified; grief-stricken. He realizes he needs to say something. He steps nervously downstage.)

HAMLET:
Friends, Danes, countrymen, lend me your ears.
I come to bury Yorick, and to praise him.
The comedy men do lives after them;
The sad is oft interrèd with their funny bones.
So let it be with Yorick.
(He turns to go, but realizes YORICK deserves so much more. As he speaks and grows more confident, he picks up the guitar left by ROSENCRANTZ and strums it idly.)
He was my friend, faithful and just to me.

He was a fellow of infinite jest;
Like brevity, he was the soul of wit:
Not only witty in himself, but the
Wonderful cause of wit in other men.
And the terms upon which he lived his life
Were his own. He died doing what he loved.
So let's not mourn here in court
Yorick warned me life is short
And we are born to learn an important lesson or three
(Singing)

```
        C
So here's my
     F
Takeaway
         C              F
Because we all will die some day
         C          F             G7
I know that I can't be who they want me to be
     Dm7          G7
The plan is not to be you
         C
I got to be me

     C
Be yourself
        F
That's the plot
       C              F
Someone else is what you're not
         C          F             G7
If someone sells you a lot of fraught philosophy
     C
Turn away
     F
You be you
        C              F
They say to thine own self be true—
```

(YORICK *enters, a ghost now, invisible to the other*
characters. He sees HAMLET *and beams with pride.* HAMLET
keeps singing.)

HAMLET:
>   C   F   G7
Because they don't get to tell you who you should be
>   Dm7   G7
The plan is not to be you
>   C
I got to be me

(YORICK *leads the audience in applause.* HAMLET *and*
OPHELIA, *not seeing* YORICK, *are surprised by the*
response.)

OPHELIA: *(Spoken, to* HAMLET*)* Hey, they really like you!
Keep going!

HAMLET: *(Singing)*
>   C   F
Because I'm an individual
> C   F
I'm an individual
(Spoken; to OPHELIA*)*
Now you.

OPHELIA: *(Singing)*
I'm an individual

(HAMLET *and* OPHELIA *sing together,* HAMLET *alternating*
between C and F chords.)

HAMLET/OPHELIA: *(Singing in harmony)*
We are individuals

YORICK: *(Spoken to the audience)* Everybody!

AUDIENCE: *(Singing)*
We are individuals

(*The audience singing takes* HAMLET *and* OPHELIA *by*
surprise.)

YORICK: *(Spoken; to the audience)* Now the ladies!

LADIES: *(Singing)*
We are individuals

YORICK: *(Spoken; to the audience)* Now the men!

MEN: *(Singing)*
We are individuals

(OPHELIA runs off to make sure THE KING sees this.)

YORICK: *(Spoken; to the audience)* Now the non-binary people!

NON-BINARY PEOPLE: *(Singing)*
We are individuals

YORICK: *(Spoken; to the audience)* Left-handed people!

LEFT-HANDED PEOPLE: *(Singing)*
We are individuals

YORICK: *(Spoken; to the audience)* Throweth thine hands into the air—!

AUDIENCE: *(Singing)*
We are individuals

YORICK: *(Spoken; to the audience)* And waveth them as if thou didst not care! Everybody!

AUDIENCE: *(They do; singing)*
We are individuals…

(YORICK gets the audience to wave their arms back and forth. HAMLET dances around like Chuck Berry.)

(THE KING enters, amazed at what he's seeing. YORICK sees him and stops the audience singing. HAMLET wonders why the audience has stopped and sees his father.)

THE KING: Look at you—getting the whole crowd to sing about individuality in total uniformity! I was right. You are a great performer.

HAMLET: Which will make me a great King.

THE KING: Oh. That backfired on me.

HAMLET: Shall we finish this together?

THE KING: Oh no. No no no, I couldn't, I'd be too
afraid…

(HAMLET *places a hand on* THE KING'S *shoulder and
touches his chest with his fist, the same distinctive gesture as
before.*)

HAMLET: There is no need for you to be afraid.

THE KING: *(Admiringly)* Oh, you little shit.

(HAMLET *plucks a G7 chord.* THE KING *girds his loins and
sings in harmony.*)

HAMLET / THE KING: *(Singing together)*
G7   C
You were right
         F
Face your fear
           C   F
And you just might persevere
             C   F   G7
Though the fight won't disappear permanently—

HAMLET: *(Spoken)* Take it!

THE KING:
  Dm7   G7
I see you need to be you
             E7 Am
And not to be me

HAMLET / THE KING:
    Dm7   G7
The plan is not to be you
         Am
I got to be me!

HAMLET: *(Spoken)* Can I get that in writing, Dad?

THE KING: Fine!

HAMLET / THE KING: *(Slowly; big finish)*
  Dm7   G7
The plan is not to be you
    F7 —> C
I got to be me!

(THE KING leads the applause [rehearsal audio and video available at BroadwayPlayPublishing.com].)

HAMLET: I wish Yorick could've seen that.

(HAMLET and THE KING start to exit. As they go:)

THE KING: Yeah, where the hell *is* Yorick?

HAMLET: We need to talk….

YORICK: *(Proudly)* That's my boy! Kept it real. Told the truth. Taught him everything he knows! *(Looking around)* 'Tis wondrous strange. I don't know why I'm still here; I should have already journeyed to that realm after death from which no traveler returns. I must have some unfinished business. Perhaps I need to forgive the king for his casual cruelty to me. I forgive you! *(Sees he's still here)* No? Or—maybe I need to be grateful for living a life that brought joy to other people. Thank you! *(Still here)* What the hell. *(L'il Yorick whispers to him.)* Of course! Thanks, L'il Dead Yorick! I can't journey to that undiscovered country until the other actors are finished making a fairly complicated costume change.

OPHELIA: *(Off)* We're ready!

(YORICK's suddenly jerked, then drawn backward.)

YORICK: *(As he's drawn off)* Oh, that did it! I'm out, bitches—!

(YORICK exits. OPHELIA enters. She's backstage.)

OPHELIA: Hurry up, Hamlet! You're on next for the final number!

(HAMLET *enters, a changed man. Like, literally: He's dressed all in black.*)

OPHELIA: (*Surprised at his outfit*) It seems you've put your nighted color on.

HAMLET: (*Confidently*)
"Seems", madam? Nay I have. I know not "seems".
This customary suit of solemn black
Does Yorick and your mother honor show.
These are the trappings and the suits of woe.

OPHELIA: But I checked the tally—we're still four hundred kroner short!

HAMLET: (*Determined and newly mature*) Fear not! That money shall be ours, for I am every inch a king!

(HAMLET *takes* OPHELIA *in his arms, but before he can kiss her we hear ghostly wind and they're blown apart.*)

LILITH: (*Entering*) Take, oh take those lips away!

HAMLET: Yes. Now *that's* a nice ghost costume!

LILITH:
There are more things in heaven and earth, Hamlet—

(*Making* HAMLET *slap himself for emphasis:*)

LILITH:
—than are *dreamt* of in *your* philosophy!
(*She's suddenly jerked and drawn backward.*)
Oh no…

OPHELIA:
              Wait! Why do you go away *now*?!

LILITH:
You must have raised your money, somehow!
If the nunnery's saved, I go—that's the plan!
Grab me, Ophelia!

OPHELIA:
              I can't!

(LILITH *extends her hand and* OPHELIA *reaches for it—and discovers she can touch it!)*

OPHELIA:

Wait, I can!

(They embrace—but LILITH *keeps getting pulled offstage.)*

LILITH:
Hear me, Ophelia! I know it's a bother,
But you and Prince Hamlet, you have the same
  father—!

(The final word fades as LILITH *disappears. But* OPHELIA *hears it.)*

OPHELIA: Whaaaa—

HAMLET: What did she say?

OPHELIA: She said we have the same *fah*— *(Deciding to spare him)* —*ondness* for each other!

HAMLET: That's great! All's well that ends.

OPHELIA: *(Dubious)* Well…

HAMLET: *(Taking her hands)* We gave your mother's spirit rest. Be happy, Ophelia!

OPHELIA: I am— *(Suddenly pulling her hands away)* —my lord.

HAMLET: My "lord"? Why so formal? I love you, Ophelia.

OPHELIA: I love you, too, my lord. Like a brother.

HAMLET: Like a brother? No no no. Doubt thou the stars are fire, doubt that the sun doth move, doubt truth to be a liar—

(We hear impatient audience stamping and clapping from "onstage".)

OPHELIA: There's no time, Hamlet. Please, the audience is waiting. No more poetry.

(OPHELIA *pushes* HAMLET *"onstage" and stands there for a moment, expressing her own frustration and confusion.*)

HAMLET: It's okay. I'll write it down.

OPHELIA: Noo—!

HAMLET: Ohh—

(OPHELIA *exits.* HAMLET *has exited through one door and now enters through the other.*)

HAMLET: —*kay*, everybody! Thank you so much for coming out tonight! Unfortunately, we're still short of our goal by just four hundred kroner, which I know is disappointing because we've worked so hard and you've all been so generous…

THE KING: (*Offstage*) Wait!! Hang on, wait just a second—! (*He runs on as soon as he's changed.*) Citizens of Elsinore—no no no, stay seated. Hamlet, my son: I must do a great right to undo my many little wrongs. (*Holds up a leather pouch*) Here is the final four hundred kroner.

HAMLET: (*Taking the pouch*) How? I thought you had no money!

THE KING: I don't, so I fired your mother's contractor and sold your uncle Claudius's castle.

HAMLET: Wow.

THE KING: Yeah. They are gonna be *super* pissed. But what are they going to do—kill me?!

(HAMLET *embraces* THE KING.)

HAMLET: Thank you, Father!

THE KING: Not at all, my boy. Now I'm off to take a nap in the orchard, which is my custom always of the afternoon.

HAMLET: Have a nice long sleep!

THE KING: (*As he goes*) I will!

HAMLET: We did it! Tonight's fundraiser is a hit, a hit, a very palpable hit!

(Recorded music starts [Rehearsal audio, video, and performance backing tracks available at BroadwayPlayPublishing.com]. HAMLET *sings.)*

HAMLET: *(Singing)*
G7-C
In summary
          Am
We saved the nunnery!
        C   Am
It needed money, we brought funny
     Dm7   G7
By the score!

We were adorable
         C
And not too horrible
       Dm7
This castle we're in right now here in
   G7
Elsinore!

   F
To you we're sending
   A7
A happy ending
   Dm7
We thank you for attending,
      G7
Spending time with us tonight!
        C
Because in summary
           A7
We saved the nunnery!
       Dm7   G7
Let's grab a beverage because every

        C
Thing's all right!

(Two nuns, SISTER EROTICA *and* SISTER LASCIVIA, *enter
and all three dance to* Hava Nagila, *do a slowed-down kick
line, and then sing the final chorus.)*

ALL:

          C
That's how in summary
          Asus7 –> A7
We saved the nunnery!
     Dm7   G7   A7
It was a practical theatrical delight—

SISTER EROTICA:
     Dm7   G7
It was slightly out of order
     Dm7   G7
And we tried to make it shorter

SISTER LASCIVIA:
       Dm7   G7
There was far too much to cram in
     Dm7   G7
But we really started jammin'

HAMLET:
     Dm7   G7
We got everybody humming
     Dm7   G7
And we thank you all for coming

ALL:
   Dm7   G7
To Hamlet's Big Adventure—
   C
—Tonight!

(Blackout. An instrumental version of "In Summary"
begins. HAMLET *and [out of their nun costumes]* OPHELIA
and YORICK *bow, then exit.)*

END OF SHOW